Prentice Hall

WRITING and GRAMMAR

Communication in Action

Prentice Hall

LITERATURE

Timeless Voices, Timeless Themes

Vocabulary and Spelling Practice Book

TEACHER'S EDITION

SILVER LEVEL

Prentice Hall

Upper Saddle River, New Jersey
Glenview, Illinois
Needham, Massachusetts

Silver

ISBN 0-13-063345-3

2 3 4 5 6 7 8 9 10   04 03 02

Contents

Vocabulary Practice 1: Prefixes

Prefixes: *a-, ab-, be-*

A prefix is a word part that is added to the beginning of a base word. A prefix changes the meaning of a word.

Example: The prefixes *a-*, and *ab-* can mean "up, out," "not," or "away." Adding *a-*, meaning "up" to the base word *rise*, makes *arise*, which means "to get up." The prefix *be-* means "near."

Combine each prefix with each base word or root. Write the new word in the blank. Then, write the letter of the meaning that belongs with each word. The first one is done for you.

Prefix	Base/Root	New Word	Letter	Meaning
ab-	duct (darkness)	1. abduct	2. f	a. having a distaste for; not inclined
ab-	hor (to shudder)	3.	4.	b. to make calm; to soothe
ab-	normal (normal)	5.	6.	c. to confuse
a-	verse (to turn)	7.	8.	d. to clothe, especially in a fancy way; to decorate
a-	vert (to turn)	9.	10.	e. to act as a friend to
be-	calm (calm)	11.	12.	f. to carry off by force; to kidnap
be-	friend (friend)	13.	14.	g. not normal
be-	fuddle (confuse)	15.	16.	h. to turn away or aside; avoid; keep off
be-	moan (moan)	17.	18.	i. to hate
be-	deck (to decorate)	19.	20.	j. to express regret over

Name _____ Date _____

Vocabulary Practice 2: Prefixes

Prefixes: *mega-, micro-*

A prefix is a word part that is added to the beginning of a base word. A prefix changes the meaning of a word.

> **Example:** The prefix *mega-* means "great," "large," or "million." Adding the prefix *mega-*, meaning "million," to the word *bucks,* makes the word *megabucks,* which means "millions of dollars." The prefix *micro-* means "very small."

A. Write the word formed by each prefix and root.

Prefix & Meaning	Root/Base & Meaning	New Word
1. *mega-* (million)	*byte* (computer unit)	
2. *mega-* (large, great)	*lith* (stone)	
3. *mega-* (large)	*phone* (sound)	
4. *mega-* (million)	*ton* (2,000 pounds)	
5. *micro-* (very small)	*be* (from *bios,* life)	
6. *micro-* (very small)	*film* (film)	
7. *micro-* (very small)	*organism* (life form)	
8. *micro-* (very small)	*phone* (sound)	
9. *micro-* (very small)	*scope* (to watch, look at)	
10. *micro-* (very small)	*wave* (wave)	

B. Write a word that you wrote for Part A that matches each meaning below.

1. 1,048,576 units of computer storage _____

2. device with a lens for making enlarged images of tiny objects _____

3. instrument that uses an electric current to transmit sound _____

4. small organism, germ _____

5. ancient monument or other large stone _____

6. device used to make the voice sound louder _____

7. explosive force equaling one million tons of TNT_____

8. reduced-size record on film of something larger _____

9. short electromagnetic wave_____

10. microorganism, germ _____

Vocabulary Practice 3: Prefixes

Prefixes: *bene-, mal-*

A prefix is a word part that is added to the beginning of a base word. A prefix changes the meaning of a word.

Example: The prefix *bene-* means "good." The prefix *mal-* means "bad." Adding *mal-* to the base word *treat* makes *maltreat,* which means "to treat badly or wrongly."

A. Add a prefix to each word below. Write a word that adds the meaning of "bad" or "badly" to each word.

1. adjusted _____
2. formed _____
3. practice _____
4. content _____
5. nutrition _____

B. Think about the meanings of each prefix and root or suffix. Then, write a definition for the word in bold type. Check your definitions in a dictionary.

1. *bene-* (good) + *factor* (doer) = **benefactor**

   Definition _____

2. *bene-* (good) + *ficial* (doing) = **beneficial**

   Definition _____

3. *bene-* (good) + *ficiary* (to do) = **beneficiary**

   Definition _____

4. *bene-* (good) + *volent* (wishing) = **benevolent**

   Definition _____

5. *mal-* (bad) + *ice* (state or condition of) = **malice**

   Definition _____

C. Choose the word that best completes each sentence. Write it in the blank.

maladjusted   malnutrition   benevolent   beneficiary   malice

1. At first the child seemed _____ in kindergarten, but later she did well.

2. It's hard not to feel _____ toward someone who has wronged you.

3. Mrs. Chin's child will be the _____ of all her hard work.

4. Mr. Wasnewski is a kindly, _____ gentleman.

5. People can be overweight and still suffer from _____.

Vocabulary Practice 4: Number Prefixes

A prefix is a word part that is added to the beginning of a base word. A prefix changes the meaning of a word.

Example: The prefix, or combining form, *centi-* means "one hundred." Adding *centi-*, which means "one hundred" to the base *pede*, which means feet, makes *centipede*, which is a word that names a small animal with many, many legs. Other combining forms also express numbers.

deca-, deci- = ten   quad- = four

octa- = eight   sex- = six

A. Write the following words in the correct category of the chart.

centennial   centimeter   century   decade   decathlon

decimal   octagonal   quadruple   sextet   sextuple

Meaning Related to Four	Meaning Related to Six	Meaning Related to Eight	Meaning Related to Ten	Meaning Related to One Hundred
1.	2.	4.	5.	8.
	3.		6.	9.
			7.	10.

B. Underline the word from Part A that appears in each of the following sentences. Then, write a number to complete each sentence.

1. An octagonal shape has _____ sides.

2. A century consists of _____ years.

3. A centennial celebrates _____ years of something's existence or success.

4. If you sextuple something, you multiply it by _____.

5. The decimal system is based on the number _____.

6. A decathlon is a competition consisting of _____ events.

7. A group of _____ members composes a sextet.

8. A meter consists of _____ centimeters.

9. A quadruple room is designed for _____ occupants.

10. There are _____ years in a decade.

Vocabulary Practice 5: Suffixes

Suffixes: *-ize, -yze*

A suffix is a word part that is added to the end of a base word. A suffix changes the meaning of the word and how it is used in a sentence.

Example: The suffix *-ate* is a verb-making suffix. The suffix *-ate* means "to make." Often, a noun can be changed into a verb by eliminating its noun-making suffix and adding the verb-making suffix *-ate*.

A. Write the adjective form of each underlined word to complete the sentence. Choose from these words.

analyze	visualize	economize	idolize	mechanize
paralyze	patronize	publicize	modernize	sympathize

1. Several people express their <u>sympathy</u> for Carlos. They _____ with him.

2. Maddy created a <u>visual</u> image of the process to help the rest of us to _____ it.

3. The bite of that insect can _____ you, but the <u>paralysis</u> is not permanent.

4. You should _____ that book store; it gives special discounts to every loyal <u>patron</u>.

5. The <u>economy</u> is good right now, but it is still wise to _____ on certain purchases.

6. I have just begun work on my <u>analysis</u>. In it, I will _____ construction patterns in our town during the last decade.

7. So many teens _____ that movie star! He is a motion picture <u>idol</u>.

8. Mary Jo plans to become a <u>mechanic</u>. She studies machines and ways to _____ the work we do.

9. That news should be made <u>public</u>. You can _____ in the local newspaper.

10. There are many <u>modern</u> buildings on this block, but I hope no one will try to _____ that old post office.

B. Write the word from Part A that matches each meaning.

1. to be a frequent or regular customer of _____

2. to create a mental picture of_____

3. to cause complete or partial loss of motion_____

4. to be careful about spending money; to spend less _____

5. to study in order to determine the nature of something_____

Vocabulary Practice 6: Adjective Suffixes

A suffix is a word part that is added to the end of a base word. A suffix changes the meaning of the word and how it is used in a sentence.

Example: Suffixes can determine the part of speech of a word. Words ending with the suffixes *-ive*, *-le*, and *-al* are usually adjectives. The suffix *-ive* means "pertaining to" and the suffixes *-le* and *-al* mean "relating to."

A. Write the adjective form of each underlined noun or verb to complete each sentence. Choose from these words.

    facial   sensual   affirmative   conclusive   gradual

1. There is a scar on Melissa's <u>face</u>. It is a _____ scar.

2. We will <u>conclude</u> the investigation, because the evidence is not _____.

3. It takes years of practice to <u>graduate</u> to the next level. Progress is _____.

4. The aroma of bread baking appeals to my <u>sense</u> of smell. Smelling fresh bread is a _____ experience.

5. The governor will <u>affirm</u> the rights of the people. Her action will be _____.

B. Think about the meaning of each word. Then, write a sentence using each word as an adjective.

1. maternal—relating to motherhood

_____

2. artificial—not natural; made by people

_____

3. agile—able to move quickly and with grace

_____

4. passive (adjective)—lacking in energy or will; not active

_____

5. volatile—likely to change rapidly; likely to explode

_____

Vocabulary Practice 7: Suffixes

Suffixes: -ment

A suffix is a word part that is added to the end of a base word. A suffix changes the meaning of the word and how it is used in a sentence.

Example: The suffix -ment is a noun-making suffix. Often, a verb can be changed into a noun by adding the suffix -ment. The verb imprison becomes the noun imprisonment by adding -ment. Some nouns that end with -ment, such as tournament, do not have related verb forms.

A. Think about the verb given in each item. Write the noun form of the verb from the list below.

achievement   acknowledgment   alignment   indictment   inducement

1. align   _____   4. induce   _____

2. indict   _____   5. achieve   _____

3. acknowledge _____

B. Write the noun in each group of related words.

1. environment   natural   protect   _____

2. decorative   ornament   examine   _____

3. annoy   sensitive   sentiment   _____

4. moody   temperament   react   _____

5. troublesome   endanger   predicament   _____

C. Write the word from Parts A and B that best completes each sentence. Use a dictionary as needed.

1. Conserving resources helps protect the _____.

2. The mechanic will check the _____ of the tires.

3. The teacher congratulated Jacques on his recent _____.

4. We hung the _____ over the doorway.

5. The _____ of the suspect did not come as a surprise.

Vocabulary Practice 8: Suffixes

Suffixes: -al

A suffix is a word part that is added to the end of a base word. A suffix changes the meaning of the word and how it is used in a sentence.

Example: The suffix -al is an adjective-making suffix. The suffix -al means "relating to." Often, a word can be changed into an adjective by adding the suffix -al. For example, the noun *music* becomes the adjective *musical* when the suffix -al is added. Often, spelling changes are also made when adding the suffix -al.

A. Add the suffix -al to each word below. Write the resulting adjective. Check the spelling by referring to this list.

commercial   confidential   controversial   financial   influential

1. influence _____   4. finance _____

2. confidence _____   5. commerce_____

3. controversy _____

B. Think about the meaning of each word below. Write a sentence containing the word. Be sure to use the word as an adjective.

1. residential—relating to an area in which people live _____

_____

2. superficial—not necessary _____

_____

3. crucial—of central importance_____

_____

4. substantial—large; forming a large part of _____

_____

5. impartial—not favoring any one person, side, or argument; fair_____

_____

Name _____ Date _____

Vocabulary Practice 9: Word Roots

Word Roots: -frac-, -rupt-

Word roots form the basic part of the word and give the word its primary meaning. Prefixes and suffixes add specific meanings to roots. If you know the meaning of a root, you can often figure out the meaning of a whole word.

> Example: The word roots -frac- and -rupt- mean "to break." Adding the suffix -tion to the root -frac- makes *fraction,* which can mean a part of a whole number, as well as some portion—or broken-off part—of a whole.

A. Think about the meanings of the roots -frac- and -rupt-. Put these meanings together with what you already know and the information given below. Come up with a definition, check it in a dictionary, and then, write it.

1. abrupt (The prefix *a*- means "out.")

   Definition _____

2. bankrupt

   Definition _____

3. corrupt (The prefix *cor*- means "with, together.")

   Definition _____

4. disrupt (The prefix *dis*- means "away.")

   Definition _____

5. erupt (The prefix *e*- means "forth.")

   Definition _____

6. fracture (The suffix *-ure* signals a noun.)

   Definition _____

7. fragment (The suffix *-ment* signals a noun.)

   Definition _____

8. infraction (The prefix *in*- means "in, into" and the suffix *-ion* signals a noun.)

   Definition _____

9. interrupt (The prefix *inter*- means "between, among.")

   Definition _____

10. rupture (The suffix *-ure* signals a noun.)

    Definition _____

B. Use each of the following words in a sentence.

corrupt   rupture   infraction   fragment   disrupt

Vocabulary Practice 10: Word Roots

Word Roots: -pond-, -posit-, -port-

Word roots form the basic part of the word and give the word its primary meaning. Prefixes and suffixes add specific meanings to roots. If you know the meaning of a root, you can often figure out the meaning of a whole word.

Example: The word roots -pond- and -posit- mean "to place" or "to put." Adding the prefix de-, meaning "down," to the root -posit- makes deposit, meaning "to place in safe keeping" or "to lay down." The word root -port- means "to carry."

A. Underline all the words with the roots -pond-, -posit-, and -port- in this passage.

composite	disposition	impostor	portable	portfolio
portly	proposition	rapport	supportive	supposition

A portly man boarded a ship. He pretended to be an artist, and he carried a large portfolio and a portable easel. Nevertheless, he was never once seen sketching or drawing. In fact, he rarely came out on deck, he had an unfriendly disposition, and he did not establish a rapport with any other passengers. One day the crew was alerted to the FBI's supposition that an international embezzler was on board. When the FBI faxed a composite sketch of the man, the crew's suspicion that the artist was actually an impostor was confirmed. The FBI's proposition for dealing with the suspect was to take no action until agents could board the ship. The crew was, of course, supportive.

B. Write each word you underlined in Part A next to its meaning.

1. capable of being carried _____

2. helpful _____

3. large carrying case for photos, pictures, or art _____

4. feeling of harmony or accord _____

5. heavy, stout _____

6. something that is supposed; hypothesis _____

7. plan, proposal _____

8. pretender _____

9. personality, emotional makeup _____

10. a whole created from parts _____

Vocabulary Practice 11: Word Roots

Word Roots: *-ject-*, *-tract-*

Word roots form the basic part of the word and give the word its primary meaning. Prefixes and suffixes add specific meanings to roots. If you know the meaning of a root, you can often figure out the meaning of a whole word.

Example: The word root *-ject-* means "to throw" or "to hurl." The word root *-tract-* means "to pull" or "to move." Adding the suffix *-or* to the root *-tract-* makes the word *tractor*, which names a kind of machine that can pull or move farm equipment and other large things.

A. Think about the meanings of the roots *-ject-* and *-tract-*. Put these meanings together with what you already know and the information given below. Come up with a definition for each word, check it in a dictionary, and then, write it.

1. contract (The prefix *con-* means "with, together.")

   Definition _____

2. dejected (The prefix *de-* means "down"; here, the suffix *-ed* signals an adjective.)

   Definition _____

3. detract (The prefix *de-* means "down.")

   Definition _____

4. distract (The prefix *dis-* means "away.")

   Definition _____

5. eject (The prefix *e-* means "forth.")

   Definition _____

6. extract (The prefix *ex-* means "out of.")

   Definition _____

7. inject (The prefix *in-* means "in, into.")

   Definition _____

8. reject (The prefix *re-* means "back.")

   Definition _____

9. retract (The prefix *re-* means "back.")

   Definition _____

10. projection (The prefix *pro-* means "forward, ahead," and the suffix *-ion* signals a noun.)

    Definition _____

B. Use the each of the following words in a sentence.

eject   projection   distract   dejected   detract

Vocabulary Practice 12: Word Roots

Word Roots: -pen-, -pend-

Word roots form the basic part of the word and give the word its primary meaning. Prefixes and suffixes add specific meanings to roots. If you know the meaning of a root, you can often figure out the meaning of a whole word.

Example: The word roots -pen- and -pend- mean "to hang" or "to weigh." Adding the suffix -ant- to -pend- makes *pendant,* which means "something that hangs." Often *pendant* is used to refer to an ornament that hangs from a necklace.

A. Think about each definition. On the line below the definition, explain how each word's meaning is related to the word root meaning "to hang" or "to weigh."

1. appendix—extra material usually attached to the end of a piece of writing

_____

2. dependable—able to be relied upon, reliable; trustworthy

_____

3. dependent—person who relies on another for financial or other support

_____

4. dispense—to give out; to prepare and distribute (as medicine)

_____

5. expendable—easier to use up or lose than to save or rescue

_____

6. expenditure—something paid for; expense

_____

7. pendulum—something hanging from a fixed point that swings freely and regularly, and may be used to regulate clocks or other devices

_____

8. pension—fixed sum paid regularly to a person

_____

9. perpendicular—at right angles to a flat plane or to the horizon; upright

_____

10. suspend—to hang; to keep waiting

_____

B. On a separate sheet of paper, write a sentence containing each of the following words.

perpendicular   expendable   dispense   pension   appendix

Vocabulary Practice 13: Word Roots

Word Roots: -cede-, -ces-, -dic-

Word roots form the basic part of the word and give the word its primary meaning. Prefixes and suffixes add specific meanings to roots. If you know the meaning of a root, you can often figure out the meaning of a whole word.

Example: The word roots -cede- and -ces- mean "to go, yield, or give away." The word root -dic- means "to speak, say, tell." Adding the noun-making suffix -tion to the root -dic- makes diction, meaning "vocal expression" or "pronunciation."

A. Underline all the words with the roots -cede-, -ces-, and -dic- in this passage.

| access | ancestor | antecedent | concede | contradict |
| dictator | predecessor | edict | indicate | intercede |

The government of the United States has Greek, Roman, and English antecedents. Although the English are our closest governmental ancestors, and Greeks are our most obvious ancient influence. Historians also always indicate the influence of Rome. In Rome, the power of the government rested—for a time—with the citizens. Of course, historians concede that not everyone had access to citizenship (this was limited to males of certain classes). Still, this does not contradict the fact that early forms of democratic bodies, such as the Roman senate and assembly, influenced our govenrment. Of course, Rome also had the first dictator. However, Roman dictators were appointed, had power for only six months, and interceded only during times of crisis. A dictator could issue edicts and exercise more power than his predecessor, but this temporary power was thought to be important for the good of the state.

B. Write each word you underlined in Part A next to its meaning.

1. permission, liberty, or ability to enter _____

2. person who has complete control over a govenrment _____

3. those from whom others are descended _____

4. preceding events, conditions, or causes _____

5. point out; state _____

6. to come between opposing people or groups _____

7. admit; give in _____

8. to say the opposite of _____

9. person who previously occupied the same position _____

10. proclamation, order, command _____

Vocabulary Practice 14: Synonyms

A synonym is a word similar to or exact in meaning to another word. Knowing synonyms will improve your vocabulary and writing.

Example: *Tint* is a synonym for *shade.*

A. Write the two words that are synonyms in each group of words below. Use a dictionary or thesaurus as needed.

1.	trite	needy	banal	_____
2.	well-to-do	poor	destitute	_____
3.	reveal	correct	divulge	_____
4.	deception	duplicity	compassion	_____
5.	hesitation	excitement	exuberance	_____
6.	reject	embrace	forswear	_____
7.	create	spoil	indulge	_____
8.	control	misdirect	monopolize	_____
9.	sensible	passionate	prudent	_____
10.	terse	persistent	tenacious	_____

B. Replace the underlined word in each sentence with a synonym from Part A.

1. Staying away from the wild animal was a <u>sensible</u> decision. _____

2. The diet study volunteers had to <u>reject</u> all junk food. _____

3. The parents were shocked by their child's <u>deception</u>. _____

4. The more <u>persistent</u> of the two candidates won. _____

5. Clichés like "dead as a doorknob" can sound <u>trite</u> in writing. _____

6. On hearing the news of the win, Deb reacted with <u>excitement</u>. _____

7. Derek has a tendency to <u>control</u> any conversation about sports. _____

8. Parents are often advised not to <u>spoil</u> their children. _____

9. The witness would not <u>reveal</u> all that she had seen. _____

10. Many people were <u>poor</u> during the Great Depression. _____

Name _____ Date _____

Vocabulary Practice 15: Synonyms

A synonym is a word similar to or exact in meaning to another word. Knowing synonyms will improve your vocabulary and writing.

Example: *Vex* is a synonym for *anger*.

A. Write the two words that are synonyms in each sentence. Use a dictionary or thesaurus as needed.

1. That was the highest point, or pinnacle, of Edison's achievement. _____

2. The creative ad was part of a new and innovative campaign. _____

3. I don't know if I can bestir gratitude, but I can at least provoke a response. _____
_____

4. Randy was gloomy, but Jacob was even more morose than Randy. _____
_____

5. Young children are vulnerable and must be kept away from places where they can be easily harmed. _____

6. When the lecturer requested a payment, she received a small stipend. _____
_____

7. The common expression "take care" has become a kind of platitude. _____
_____

8. If you tarry, you may delay the entire team. _____

9. Adulation from critics is the director's favorite kind of praise. _____
_____

10. The guard thought the boy's question was impertinent, but he had not intended to be rude.
_____

B. Write a word you wrote in Part A to complete each group of related words.

1. top, highest point, climax, _____

2. gloomy, glum, unhappy, _____

3. rude, sassy, impolite, _____

4. delay, linger, procrastinate, _____

5. compensation, consideration, payment, _____

6. cliché, common expression, triteness, _____

7. attackable, easily harmed, unprotected, _____

8. cause, provoke, work up, _____

9. acclaim, applause, praise, _____

10. creative, inventive, ingenious, _____

Vocabulary Practice 16: Synonyms

A synonym is a word similar to or exact in meaning to another word. Knowing synonyms will improve your vocabulary and writing.

Example: *Greatest* is a synonym for *maximum*.

A. Next to each word, write its synonym from the list below. Use a dictionary or thesaurus as needed.

cajole	censure	cower	delete	erroneous
fervid	forage	mundane	repel	prodigious

1. incorrect _____
2. enthusiastic _____
3. remove _____
4. drive off _____
5. shrink away _____

6. search _____
7. disapproval _____
8. common _____
9. urge _____
10. huge _____

B. Write words from Part A to complete each analogy below.

1. *Piercing* is to *sharp* as *common* is to _____.
2. *Go forward* is to *shrink away* as *approach* is to _____.
3. *Compliment* is to *disapproval* as *praise* is to _____.
4. *Unwanted* is to *remove* as *unnecessary* is to _____.
5. *Pull toward* is to *drive away* as *attract* is to _____.
6. *Error* is to *incorrect in* as *mistake* is to _____.
7. *Tiny* is to *minuscule* as *huge* is to _____.
8. *Move* is to *migrate* as *search* is to _____.
9. *Persuade* is to *convince* as *urge* is to _____.
10. *Fan* is to *enthusiastic* as *admirer* is to _____.

Vocabulary Practice 17: Antonyms

An antonym is a word that is opposite in meaning to another word. Knowing antonyms will improve your vocabulary and writing.

Example: *Let go* is an antonym for *restrain*.

A. Read each pair of sentences. Complete the second sentence by writing the word from the list that is an antonym for the underlined word or words in the first sentence.

dilute	dormant	eminent	enmity	flippant
lenient	lethargic	pertinent	puerile	vulgar

1. Many of my most <u>energetic</u> friends are in the runners' club.

   I felt too _____ to join their six-mile runs.

2. The editor wanted to cut the information she felt was <u>unnecessary</u>.

   The author argued that the information was _____ to the article.

3. Tourists exclaim over the gracious, <u>tasteful</u> interiors at the White House.

   There are no _____ touches in the decoration there.

4. Most of the students reacted to the opera in a <u>mature</u> way.

   Only a few displayed _____ behavior.

5. Always try to be <u>respectful</u> of other people's religions.

   In respect to people's faith, never display a _____ attitude.

6. The woman felt an intense <u>love</u> for those who had helped her children.

   Feelings of _____ overtook her when she thought of those who had hurt them.

7. If you want to <u>strengthen</u> the solution, add more ammonia.

   If you want to _____ it, add more water.

8. You should not prune or cut back most shrubs during periods of <u>active</u> growth.

   Instead, wait until the shrub is _____, which is usually in winter.

9. At first, the principal was <u>unforgiving</u> about the graffiti in the hall.

   When an effort was made to remove it, the principal became more _____.

10. The recent discovery was made by an <u>unknown</u> researcher.

   Several _____ researchers had been working on the same problem without success.

B. Write an antonym for each word that is different from the antonym used in Part A. Check your answers in a thesaurus or dictionary.

1. energetic _____
2. unnecessary _____
3. mature _____
4. love _____
5. tasteful _____

Vocabulary Practice 18: Antonyms

An antonym is a word that is opposite in meaning to another word. Knowing antonyms will improve your vocabulary and writing.

Example: *Praise* is an antonym for *denounce.*

A. Write the two words that are antonyms in each sentence.

1. When Amy completed the task, she expected to be met with an embrace rather than with a rebuff. _____

2. Some found the art appealing while others regarded it as repugnant. _____

   _____

3. The same actions can prove to be foolish in one situation but sage in another. _____

   _____

4. Sometimes when you befriend one person, you alienate another. _____

5. From the children's point of view, the theme park was entertaining, but, from the adults' point of view, it was tedious. _____

6. The building materials for the walls must be completely opaque; do not use anything trans-parent. _____

7. Only Mrs. DiMenna remained serene; all the other applicants were quite obviously nervous.

   _____

8. If left in the sun, the material will become rigid, but soaking it in water will make it pliable again. _____

9. Candy's actions were meant to please her brother, but instead they seemed to antagonize him. _____

10. Because Zach wanted a frank answer to his question, the slow, careful response he got sounded insincere._____

B. Replace the underlined word in each sentence with an antonym from Part A.

1. The idea of swimming in that lake was quite appealing. _____

2. Be careful not to befriend the wrong people. _____

3. The embrace was not the response that Eliza had been expecting. _____

4. Mark's nervous attitude made him stand out in the group. _____

5. Everyone recalled the foolish words of the guest speaker._____

Vocabulary Practice 19 : Homophones

Homophones are words that are pronounced alike but have different spellings and meanings.

Example: The words *stationary* and *stationery* have different spellings but the same pronunciation. *Stationary* is an adjective meaning "staying in the same place." *Stationery* is paper used for a specific purpose, often letter writing.

A. You can use memory devices to help you learn the differences between homophones. For example, you might remember that both *stationery* and *paper* contain *er*. Read the definition for each word. Then, make up a memory device of your own for remembering one word in the pair. Write it on the line below each pair of words.

1. **aisle**—a passage, often separating sections of seats; **isle**—island

_____

2. **canvas**—firm, closely woven cloth used for sails, as a surface for painting, and for other purposes; **canvass**—to gather opinions or support from all those in a specific district

_____

3. **council**—an assembly or meeting; a group appointed for an advisory or law-making role; **counsel**—advise; one who gives advice, especially a lawyer

_____

4. **faint**—to lose consciousness temporarily; feeling weak or dizzy; **feint**—a mock blow or attack that draws attention away from the intended point of attack

_____

5. **peer**—one who has equal standing with another; **pier**—structure that juts out into the water that may be a place for fishing, landing a boat, or walking

_____

B. Complete each of the following sentences with the correct word from Part A.

1. Because she had not eaten for two days, Eliza felt _____ when she awoke.

2. The _____ was severely damaged in the hurricane.

3. Tom does not seek advice from his parents; instead, he looks to his _____, Jamal.

4. The _____ discussed the likely effects of the proposed new law.

5. The candidate is looking for people to _____ our neighborhood.

6. The accused woman and her _____ entered the courtroom.

7. The usher led people down the _____ of the dark auditorium.

8. A vacation on a small _____ sounds attractive to many people.

9. Let's cover this equipment with some _____.

10. In a sword competition, the ability to _____ can make all the difference.

Vocabulary Practice 20: Homophones

Homophones are words that are pronounced alike but have different spellings and meanings.

Example: The words *aid* and *aide* have different spellings but the same pronunciation. *Aid* is a noun or verb meaning "helper" or "to help." An aide is a person who gives help, often a professional, such as a nurse or teacher.

A. Read the definition for each word. Then, write a sentence in which you use each word.

1. **assent**—agreement; **ascent**—movement upward

   a. _____

   b. _____

2. **bazaar**—marketplace; fair for the sale of articles, especially for charity; **bizarre**—extremely strange

   c. _____

   d. _____

3. **cannon**—large, heavy gun, often mounted on a carriage; **canon**—an authoritative list, as of literature; a body of rules, standards, or norms

   e. _____

   f. _____

4. **complement**—to go well with together; something that completes something else; **compliment**—praise

   g. _____

   h. _____

5. **gorilla**—ape of western Africa; **guerrilla**—fighter who is part of an independent unit rather than part of the military establishment

   i. _____

   j. _____

B. Complete each of the following sentences with the correct word from Part A.

1. We found these unusual brass candlesticks at the _____.

2. Beans form a protein _____ with rice.

3. Mozart's works are always mentioned in the _____ of great music.

4. The leaders gave their _____ to the treaty, and everyone signed.

5. You can see a _____ at the San Diego Zoo.

Name _____ Date _____

Vocabulary Practice 21: Analogies

An analogy is a relationship between a pair of words. Analogies show relationships between two pairs of words.

A. You have studied several types of analogies: *synonyms, antonyms, function, cause-effect, part to whole,* and *type of* relationships. Determine the relationship in the first pair of words. Then, choose the word that completes the analogy.

1. PHARMACY : DRUGSTORE :: CAROUSEL : _____

   a. entertainment   b. horses   c. merry-go-round

2. PROHIBIT : ALLOW :: ENLARGE : _____

   a. shrink   b. photograph   c. expand

3. CHAUFFEUR : DRIVE :: PILOT : _____

   a. helicopter   b. fly   c. airborne

4. SURGEON : DOCTOR :: SEDAN : _____

   a. automobile   b. accident   c. drive

5. SHOVEL : HOLE :: GLUE : _____

   a. loosen   b. paste   c. attachment

6. FLUE : CHIMNEY :: PISTON : _____

   a. combustion   b. gasoline   c. engine

7. PHARAOH : RULER :: TORNADO : _____

   a. storm   b. hurricane   c. summer

8. VETERINARIAN : HEAL :: THERMOMETER : _____

   a. fall   b. measure   c. chill

9. MONGOOSE : MAMMAL :: GRANITE : _____

   a. marker   b. mineral   c. headstone

10. PERMANENT : TEMPORARY :: PURIFIED : _____

    a. polluted   b. water   c. safe

B. Choose the word pair that completes the following analogies.

1. REMARKABLE : USUAL :: _____

   a. soggy: flooded   b. constructive: damaging   c. player: victory

2. VIRUS : FLU :: _____

   a. senseless: foolish   b. ill: medicine   c. mole: tunnel

3. SPECULATE : GUESS :: _____

   a. notify: tell   b. invest: stock   c. provoke: insult

4. KINDERGARTEN : SCHOOL :: _____

   a. teacher: instructor   b. story: fiction   c. steeple: church

5. JOKE : ENTERTAIN :: _____

   a. despair: delight   b. comic: comedian   c. lesson: teach

C. Beside each analogy in Exercises A, write the type of analogy given.

Vocabulary Practice 22: Connotations

A connotation is the meaning suggested by a word or phrase. It is different from the denotation, or dictionary definition. Connotations can hint at meanings that are not stated directly. Connotation may be positive, neutral, or negative depending on the context.

Example: The words *skinny* and *slender* both mean "lean" or "thin." Yet their connotations are different. *Slender* has positive or neutral connotations, while *skinny*, which can imply unattractive thinness, has negative connotations.

A. Complete the sentences with two of the words given. Write a sentence using the third word to convey its connotation. Use a dictionary or thesaurus if necessary.

1. Words that mean "not any extreme" are *average, mediocre,* and *normal.*

   a. Jason loves math, so his _____ test performance surprised the teacher.

   b. Such cold weather is just not _____ for June!

   c. _____

2. Three words that describe how something smells are *aromatic, pungent,* and *strong.*

   d. That chemical is so _____ that it made my eyes water.

   e. The perfumed scene came from one small bowl filled with _____ herbs.

   f. _____

3. Words that connote "a pattern or hue" include *colorful, gaudy,* and *vivid.*

   g. I sometimes wear subdued patterns, but that one is too _____ for me.

   h. Since your suit is dull gray, you should wear a _____ tie.

   i. _____

4. Words that connote "a state in decision making" include *open-minded, undecided,* and *wavering.*

   j. I first thought that this answer was correct, but now I'm _____.

   k. You will enjoy your trip if you remain _____ about new customs.

   l. _____

5. Words that connote "a person's reputation" are *famous, notorious,* and *well-known.*

   m. Wasn't he a _____ criminal?

   n. My sister is a _____ newspaper columnist.

   o. _____

B. On another sheet of paper, write another word with the same meaning and a different connotation to add to each group of italicized words in Part A.

Vocabulary Practice 23: Commonly Misused Words

A good vocabulary allows you to use the right words when you speak and write. Many words sound alike and cause confusion if not used correctly.

Example: The words *moral* and *morale* are often used incorrectly. *Moral* means "virtuous" or "capable or knowing right from wrong." *Morale* refers to someone's spirits, as shown by confidence, cheerfulness, and willingness.

A. Read the definition for each pair of words. Then, complete each sentence with the correct word.

1. **affect**—to influence or act upon; **effect**—a result

   a. Not even rainy weather can _____ my mood today.

   b. Since the drought was short, it had no _____ on the apple crop.

2. **appraise**—to evaluate or judge; **apprise**—to give notice to, inform

   a. The school will _____ parents of any changes in class assignment.

   b. Before it lends money for home improvements, the bank will _____ the property.

3. **adverse**—harmful or unfavorable; **averse**—having a feeling of distaste; not inclined to

   a. The leaders of our group were not _____ to making one small detour.

   b. A lack of sleep can have _____ consequences for your health.

4. **confidant**—one to whom secrets are disclosed; **confident**—sure of success; bold

   a. I really have only one _____, my best friend.

   b. Selena has trained for this race for weeks and certainly looks _____.

5. **defer**—to put off or postpone; **differ**—to be unlike in some way

   a. Many people _____ marriage until they finish their education.

   b. The twins look alike, but they _____ in two important ways.

6. **descent**—a way down or a slope; **dissent**—disagreement or difference of opinion

   a. Going up the mountain was easy, but the _____ was in darkness.

   b. In a free country, people are allowed to voice their _____.

7. **detract**—to take away from; **distract**—to pull away from the original focus of attention

   a. The radio is turned down, so it will not _____ me from my homework.

   b. That rumpled shirt will certainly _____ from your overall neatness.

8. **respectfully**—showing honor or respect; **respectively**—singly in the order mentioned

   a. When the judge speaks to you, answer honestly and _____.

   b. My mother and I are _____ coach and goalie.

9. **conscience**—a source of moral judgment; **conscious**—aware

   a. Arden returned my wallet before I was _____ of even losing it.

   b. In new situations, your _____ can often help you decide right from wrong.

10. **access**—a way of entering or exiting; **excess**—a surplus; more than normal or necessary

    a. Our garden is so large that we always have _____ tomatoes for the neighbors.

    b. This fire door provides _____ only in emergency situations.

Name _____ Date _____

Vocabulary Practice 24: Commonly Confused Words

A good vocabulary allows you to use words correctly in speaking and writing. Many words sound alike and cause confusion if not used correctly.

Example: The words *desert* and *dessert* are often used incorrectly. A *desert* is place with little rain. A *dessert* is a food that comes at the end of a meal.

A. Read the definition for each pair of words. Then, use one word to complete the sentence, and write a sentence using the remaining word.

1. **flagrant**—noticeably bad or offensive; **fragrant**—having a pleasant odor

   a. Those yard sale signs are in _____ violation of the new sign by-law.

   b. _____

2. **sympathy**—a feeling of pity or sorrow; **symphony**—an extended piece of music

   a. That composer created only one major _____ during his lifetime.

   b. _____

3. **sculptor**—one who produces sculptural artwork; **sculpture**—a three-dimensional work of art

   a. Before carving the mountain, the _____ made a small model of the piece.

   b. _____

4. **static**—random noise, such as crackling; **statistic**—a numerical value; a typical number

   a. My radio batteries may be low, since I hear nothing but _____.

   b. _____

5. **recent**—occurring at a time just before the present; **resent**—to feel ill will as a result of a real or imagined grievance

   a. My first race was awful, but I won the most _____ one.

   b. _____

6. **appalling**—causing dismay or frightful; **appealing**—attractive or interesting

   a. I was awakened by the most _____ sound, but it was only a screech owl.

   b. _____

7. **empire**—a large political territory; **umpire**—a person who referees or judges games

   a. The players quickly learned never to argue with the _____.

   b. _____

8. **partition**—something that divides, such as a wall; **petition**—a formal written request

   a. Before that _____ was added, these two classrooms were one big room.

   b. _____

9. **precede**—to come before in order or rank; **proceed**—to go forward or continue

   a. After the intermission, the play will _____ to the end.

   b. _____

10. **persecute**—to oppress or harass with ill-treatment; **prosecute**—to initiate court action against

    a. Although supervisors may fire poor workers, they cannot _____ them.

    b. _____

Vocabulary Practice 25: Specialized Vocabulary

A basic understanding of health terms helps you read a newspaper, interpret medical articles, and understand medical issues that are discussed and debated.

A. Complete each sentence with a word from the list. Use a dictionary as necessary.

amnesia	antidote	cardiac	communicable
contagious	dehydration	epidemic	hygiene
immunization	inoculation	insomnia	medication
quarantine	sedative	sterile	ulcer

1. A doctor will _____ someone if they want that person to have no visitors.

2. A _____ problem is a problem that involves the heart.

3. To calm someone, a doctor might prescribe a _____.

4. An operating room must be _____ so that germs do not infect the wound.

5. Scurvy is caused by diet, so it is not _____.

6. Spicy foods will cause pain when you have an _____ in your mouth, throat, or stomach.

7. Your doctor can give you a _____ that will help you breathe more easily.

8. The quickest treatment for mild _____ is several glasses of water.

9. In case of accidental poisoning, look on the label to learn the _____.

10. People who cannot sleep have _____.

11. Once, the standard _____ for smallpox was cowpox, a milder disease.

12. The common cold is a highly _____ disease.

13. Good _____ includes washing your hands before eating.

14. Your _____ record has been updated to show your last two booster shots.

15. My whole family got sick during the flu _____ last winter.

16. The woman cannot remember the accident, because she has _____.

B. Each question contains at least one vocabulary word. Answer each question by writing yes or no on the line.

1. If you had insomnia, would a sedative be likely to help? _____

2. Does good hygiene help prevent the spread of contagious illnesses? _____

3. Is amnesia an antidote for cardiac problems? _____

4. Might a doctor quarantine someone who had a communicable disease? _____

5. Is an ulcer a type of medication? _____

Vocabulary Practice 26: Specialized Vocabulary

Having a basic understanding of money and banking terms can help you read newspaper articles, understand financial information, and participate in classroom discussions.

assets	collateral	cosigner	creditor
currency	debit	foreclose	interest
liability	lien	usury	withdrawal

A. Match the words on this list with their definitions, using a dictionary as necessary.

_____   1. a legal claim on a property until a debt is paid

_____   2. another person who has signed a loan or document

_____   3. money paid for the use of money

_____   4. an item of debt that is shown in an account

_____   5. property to be used as security for a loan

_____   6. removal from

_____   7. money in any form

_____   8. the lending of money at an unlawful or very high interest rate

_____   9. any financial obligation, such as money owed or an unpaid bill

_____   10. any property owned that could be used to settle debts

_____   11. to take away the right to pay off a mortgage

_____   12. one who is owed money

B. Complete each sentence below with a word from this list. Then, write a definition of the term below the sentence. Use a dictionary as needed.

annuity	maturity	investment	unsecured	diversified

1. Instead of buying only one company's stock, develop a _____ group of stocks.

   _____

2. You will be guaranteed a regular income if you purchase this _____.

   _____

3. A savings bond is considered a very safe, low-risk _____.

   _____

4. If you need to borrow money, the rate may be higher because you own nothing, so the loan is _____.

   _____

5. This bond will be worth a hundred dollars only if you keep it until _____.

   _____

Vocabulary Practice 27: Specialized Vocabulary

Having a basic understanding of French words helps when reading novels, during travel, and participating in different activities.

A. Complete each sentence with a word from the list. Use a dictionary as necessary.

blaséé	boutique	chaperone	charade
debris	debut	entree	fillet
gourmet	intrigue	masquerade	mirage
naive	rendezvous	resume	souvenir

1. My cousin is a _____ cook, so dinner was superb.

2. A neat, attractive _____ can help you get the job of your dreams.

3. I will attend the _____ dressed as a five-star general.

4. Although you think you see a puddle of water, it's only a _____.

5. Sports card dealers may offer you little if they think you are _____ about prices.

6. The soldiers agreed to _____ at the barracks at three o'clock sharp.

7. This performance marks Pat's _____ as a singer.

8. Although bones are supposed to add taste to fish, I still prefer a _____.

9. I bought this outfit at a small _____ in Miami.

10. The mystery was filled with wonderful characters and much _____.

11. The clerk said "Sorry," but his expression showed that the apology was just a

    _____.

12. When we left the shore, I brought home a big clamshell as a _____.

13. Tanya is trying to appear _____, but she is actually excited.

14. Please bring the salad at the same time that you serve the _____.

15. Every group of six students needs an adult _____ on this field trip.

16. The workers will remove the _____ from the old shed after the new

    one is finished.

B. Each question contains at least one vocabulary word. Answer each question by writing yes or no on the line.

1. Is a blasé person in a state of fright? _____

2. Could a boutique sell gourmet food? _____

3. Might two friends want to rendezvous at a masquerade? _____

4. Would a fillet ever be a suitable entree? _____

5. Could a mirage be a lasting souvenir of a trip? _____

Vocabulary Practice 28: Specialized Vocabulary

A basic understanding of history terms helps when reading a novel or short story, skimming a newspaper, or talking about world events.

A. Complete each sentence with a word from the list. Use a dictionary as necessary.

abdicate	amnesty	anarchy	antiquity	coalition
coup	despot	inauguration	neutrality	pacifist

1. What a _____ it was to get the support of the runner-up in the election.

2. No elections were held when that _____ was in power.

3. People have followed that custom since _____, so it would be hard to change.

4. When he said that he would _____, the country began looking for a new king.

5. Not wishing to take sides and be pulled into the war, the country declared its _____.

6. Three of the major businesses formed a _____ to discuss fair practices.

7. Anyone who was a genuine _____ could work in a hospital instead of entering combat.

8. Will the government grant _____ to soldiers who deserted for family reasons?

9. The country will be in a state of _____ unless the new government acts firmly.

10. The president will not actually take power until after the _____.

B. Match the words on this list with their definitions, using a dictionary as necessary.

contemporary	depose	disarmament	dynasty
feudalism	medieval	renaissance	totalitarian

_____ 1. a series of rulers who belong to the same family

_____ 2. relating to or belonging to the Middle Ages

_____ 3. remove from power or from the throne

_____ 4. relating to a government made up of a single group that maintains or tries to maintain absolute control over most aspects of life

_____ 5. the act of laying down weapons and arms

_____ 6. belonging to the same time period or age

_____ 7. a political, social, and economic system in the Middle Ages

_____ 8. a revival or a rebirth, usually of culture and art

Vocabulary Practice 29: Specialized Vocabulary

Having a basic understanding of geography words helps when reading adventure stories, during travel, and when discussing news stories.

A. Complete each sentence with a word from the list. Use a dictionary as necessary.

arid	cartographer	delta	fjord
irrigation	isthmus	mesa	nomad
plateau	prairie	reservoir	seismology
tundra	uninhabitable	urban	

1. Traveling by boat may be the best way to photograph a _____.

2. The sides of the _____ were so steep we didn't even try to climb it.

3. Although that land area appears to be an island at high tide; at low tide, an _____ connects it to the mainland.

4. Since the city was built on top of a _____, it was easy to defend.

5. The _____ at the end of the Mississippi River took many years to form.

6. The city never ran out of water after the _____ was built.

7. This map was made by an early _____, so it may not be very accurate.

8. Few people live on the frozen _____ in northern Canada.

9. This area was once dry and dusty, but _____ turned it into a garden.

10. Rural areas are shown in green, while _____ areas are shown in yellow.

11. A desert is always _____, but it is not always hot; some are cold.

12. Since there is neither water nor fertile soil, the island is really _____.

13. People who lived on the _____ years ago say that it was a sea of grass.

14. Someone familiar with _____ can tell you when the last major earthquake occurred.

15. My cousin lives like a _____, never staying anywhere for more than a few months.

B. Each question contains at least one vocabulary word. Answer each question by writing yes or no on the line.

1 Are the tundra and the prairie both large and treeless? _____

2. Is a reservoir usually arid? _____

3. Is a nomad someone who studies seismology? _____

4. Would you expect a fjord or an isthmus to be near water? _____

5. Is a mesa similar to a plateau? _____

Spelling Practice 1: Short and Long Vowel Spellings

Short and long vowel sounds may be spelled several ways. Always note the spelling.

Examples: The words *head* and *held* use different spellings for the short e sound. The word *speedy* uses two different spellings for the long e sound.

A. Listen for the vowel sounds in each word. If you hear any long vowel sound in the word, write the word in the Long Vowel column. Circle the letters that stand for the long vowel sound. Write words that contain only short vowel sounds in the Short Vowel column.

Word	Long Vowel	Short Vowel
1. acquaint		
2. cease		
3. clutter		
4. conceal		
5. ebony		
6. erode		
7. evaporate		
8. grateful		
9. hectic		
10. humid		
11. hydrant		
12. impeach		
13. intelligent		
14. leaflet		
15. measles		
16. mimic		
17. phantom		
18. portray		
19. promote		
20. pulse		

B. In each group of words, one word is spelled incorrectly. Underline the incorrectly spelled words and write them correctly in the space provided.

1. ebony	conseal	hectic	shingle	_____
2. mimic	intelligent	erode	evaperate	_____
3. impeech	clutter	grateful	pulse	_____
4. leaflet	phantom	aquaint	stamina	_____
5. hydrant	promote	shceme	erode	_____
6. cease	strengthen	humid	trincket	_____

Spelling Practice 2: Digraphs

A digraph is a pair of letters that spells one sound. Digraphs are neither long nor short vowel sounds. They can be spelled several ways. Always note the spelling.

Examples: The digraph *aw* spells the vowel sound that you hear at the beginning of the word *awkward*. The digraph *au* spells the same vowel sound in *faucet*.

A. Determine whether or not each word is spelled correctly. Spell incorrect words correctly. Write the correct spelling of the vowel digraph that was misspelled originally.

Word	Word Spelled Correctly	Digraph
1. aukward	_____	_____
2. booster	_____	_____
3. bough	_____	_____
4. cartune	_____	_____
5. cawliflower	_____	_____
6. chowder	_____	_____
7. compownd	_____	_____
8. deploi	_____	_____
9. devower	_____	_____
10. diloot	_____	_____
11. duplex	_____	_____
12. fawcet	_____	_____
13. flownder	_____	_____
14. growchy	_____	_____
15. hawghty	_____	_____
16. hoyst	_____	_____
17. intrude	_____	_____
18. issoo	_____	_____
19. noysy	_____	_____
20. profownd	_____	_____

B. Write a word from the list in Part A that rhymes with each word below.

1. The word **louder** rhymes with _____.

2. The word **complex** rhymes with _____.

3. The word **subdued** rhymes with _____.

4. The word **rooster** rhymes with _____.

5. The word **salute** rhymes with _____.

Spelling Practice 3: Vowels Before *r*

A vowel sound before *r* does not give a clear clue to the spelling. Always note the spelling of these vowels.

Examples: The word *dirt* and *hurt* have the same vowel sound, but the letters that stand for this sound are different in each word.

A. Sort the words below according to the vowel that comes before *r*. Write them in the correct categories. Some words fit into more than one category.

authority	carpenter	carpeting	carton	detergent
dirty	disturbance	dormitory	flourish	forfeit
furnace	furthermore	glorious	impaired	insert
inverted	malaria	mercy	merely	mortar
partial	porpoise	scar	superb	varnish

Words containing *ar*

1. _____ 2. _____ 3. _____
4. _____ 5. _____ 6. _____
7. _____ 8. _____

Words containing *er*

9. _____ 10. _____ 11. _____
12. _____ 13. _____ 14. _____
15. _____

Words containing *or*

16. _____ 17. _____ 18. _____
19. _____ 20. _____ 21. _____
22. _____

Words containing *ir* or *ur* or a digraph plus *r*

23. _____ 24. _____ 25. _____
26. _____ 27. _____ 28. _____

B. Write any six words not shown above that contain a vowel sound before *r*.

_____ _____ _____
_____ _____ _____

Spelling Practice 4: Double and Single Consonants

Consonant sounds may be spelled with one or two letters. Many words use a doubled consonant to stand for a single sound.

Examples: The words *rip* and *ripple* spell the same sound two different ways. The word *rip* spells the sound with a single letter, while *ripple* uses a doubled letter.

A. Look at the spelling of each word below. If the word contains one doubled consonant, write the word in the column labeled **One**. If the word contains two doubled consonants, write the word in the column labeled **Two**.

Word	One	Two
1. aggravate	_____	_____
2. assassin	_____	_____
3. boycott	_____	_____
4. broccoli	_____	_____
5. channel	_____	_____
6. committee	_____	_____
7. embarrass	_____	_____
8. exaggerate	_____	_____
9. excess	_____	_____
10. immense	_____	_____
11. innocent	_____	_____
12. mattress	_____	_____
13. mayonnaise	_____	_____
14. occasion	_____	_____
15. occurrence	_____	_____
16. pennant	_____	_____
17. possession	_____	_____
18. procession	_____	_____
19. recommend	_____	_____
20. scissors	_____	_____

B. In each group of words, one word is spelled incorrectly. Underline the incorrectly spelled words and write them correctly in the space provided.

1. exaggerate	asassin	innocent	procession	_____
2. pennant	aggravate	occasion	comittee	_____
3. embarras	scissors	boycott	mattress	_____
4. tariff	broccoli	occurence	excess	_____
5. channel	tresspass	territory	recommend	_____

Spelling Practice 5: Compound Words

Two or more words can sometimes be combined to form a new word called a compound. Some compound words have a hyphen or space between the words.

Examples: The words *background*, *back-to-back*, and *backyard* are all compounds.

A. Determine whether or not each word is spelled correctly. Spell incorrect words correctly in the first column. Then write each word that makes the compound in a separate column.

	Correct Spelling	Words that combine to make compound		
1. backpack	_____	_____	_____	_____
2. behive	_____	_____	_____	_____
3. breakthrugh	_____	_____	_____	_____
4. breifcase	_____	_____	_____	_____
5. copyright	_____	_____	_____	_____
6. countdown	_____	_____	_____	_____
7. dinning room	_____	_____	_____	_____
8. double-cross	_____	_____	_____	_____
9. far-fetched	_____	_____	_____	_____
10. keyboard	_____	_____	_____	_____
11. newstand	_____	_____	_____	_____
12. nontheless	_____	_____	_____	_____
13. notwithstanding	_____	_____	_____	_____
14. out-of-date	_____	_____	_____	_____
15. oversihgt	_____	_____	_____	_____
16. quick-witted	_____	_____	_____	_____
17. sadlebag	_____	_____	_____	_____
18. self-esteem	_____	_____	_____	_____
19. self-taght	_____	_____	_____	_____
20. study hall	_____	_____	_____	_____

B. In each sentence, one word is spelled incorrectly. Underline the incorrectly spelled words and write them correctly below the sentences.

1. Just leave your backpack in the dining-room.

2. During the next studyhall, please check the copyright date on the textbook.

3. The computer in this briefcase has its own keybord.

4. A quickwitted teenager saved the dog from the fire.

5. Nonetheless, most of the artists that I interviewed were self taught.

6. The newsstand sells out-of-date magazines for only three fourths of the original price.

Spelling Practice 6: Unstressed Endings

Many words end with an unstressed syllable. The vowel sounds in these syllables may be spelled in different ways. Final unstressed vowel sounds do not give a clear clue to their spelling. Always note the spelling of these sounds.

Examples: The words *ankle* and *quarrel* end with the same vowel sound, but it is not spelled the same way in the two words.

A. Sort the words below according to the spelling of the final vowel sound.

authority	carpenter	carpeting	carton	detergent
ankle	arrival	article	author	beetle
betrayal	conqueror	decimal	editorial	entangle
hustle	industrial	journal	liberal	manual
mirror	original	quarrel	rational	scholar
spectacular	startle	steeple	uncertain	wrestle

Words ending in *al*

1. _____   2. _____   3. _____
4. _____   5. _____   6. _____
7. _____   8. _____   9. _____
10. _____

Words ending in *le*

11. _____   12. _____   13. _____
14. _____   15. _____   16. _____
17. _____   18. _____

Words ending in *ar, el, in,* or *or*

19. _____   20. _____   21. _____
22. _____   23. _____   24. _____
25. _____

B. In each group of words, one word is spelled incorrectly. Underline the incorrectly spelled words and write them correctly in the space provided.

1. steeple, maneul, wrestle, rational   _____

2. liberal, ankle, industrial, auther   _____

3. startle, quarrle, conqueror, journal   _____

4. decimel, article, uncertain, hustle   _____

5. scholar, arrivel, editorial, betrayal   _____

6. entangle, spectacular, original, mirrer   _____

Spelling Practice 7: Syllable Patterns

Break longer words into syllables and spell the words by parts. Many words follow certain patterns and divide into syllables in certain ways. Look for these patterns:

Syllable Patterns with Examples:

2 consonants between two vowels (VCCV)—mir/ror
1 consonant between two vowels; first vowel is long (longVCV)—to/tal
1 consonant between two vowels; first vowel is short (short VCV)—mod/ern

A. Determine whether or not each word is spelled correctly. Spell incorrect words correctly. Write the pattern shown in parentheses above that applies to each word. Check your spelling in a dictionary.

Spelling Word	Correct Spelling	Syllable Pattern
1. plungir	_____	_____
2. boenus	_____	_____
3. campis	_____	_____
4. commute	_____	_____
5. crimzon	_____	_____
6. culprit	_____	_____
7. devowt	_____	_____
8. doner	_____	_____
9. endure	_____	_____
10. essay	_____	_____
11. excuze	_____	_____
12. fatal	_____	_____
13. gallep	_____	_____
14. napkin	_____	_____
15. ponder	_____	_____
16. quotea	_____	_____
17. rumer	_____	_____
18. rustic	_____	_____
19. slogin	_____	_____
20. saspense	_____	_____

B. Write any nine words not shown above that follow the same vowel patterns:

VC/CV   _____   _____   _____

long V/CV   _____   _____   _____

short VC/V   _____   _____   _____

Name _____ Date _____

Spelling Practice 8: Adding Suffixes

The spelling of some words changes when a suffix is added. A letter may be dropped, changed, or doubled. In some cases, the form of the base word may change.

Examples:

dropped letter: surprise + ing = surprising
changed letter: worry + es = worries
doubled letter: unpin + ed = unpinned
changed form: vision + ible = visible

A. Determine whether or not each word is spelled correctly. Spell incorrect words correctly. Write the word and the suffix that were combined to make the spelling word. Check your spelling in a dictionary.

Spelling Word	Correct Spelling	Word + Suffix
1. acquited	_____	_____
2. bubbling	_____	_____
3. certifyed	_____	_____
4. challengeing	_____	_____
5. comedyian	_____	_____
6. controlling	_____	_____
7. corroded	_____	_____
8. criticized	_____	_____
9. democratic	_____	_____
10. denyed	_____	_____
11. divisible	_____	_____
12. evolveing	_____	_____
13. fascinating	_____	_____
14. historical	_____	_____
15. mystifyed	_____	_____
16. occupied	_____	_____
17. patroling	_____	_____
18. pitied	_____	_____
19. pledgeing	_____	_____
20. prefered	_____	_____

B. Add to the list in Part A three more words that have suffixes. After each word, write the base word and the suffix that was added.

_____

_____

_____

Spelling Practice 9: More Unstressed Endings

Final unstressed vowel sounds do not give a clear clue to their spelling. Always note the spelling of these sounds.

Examples: The words *insurance* and *audience* end with the same vowel sound, but it is not spelled the same way in the two words.

A. Sort the words below according to the spelling of the final vowel sound.

absence	adolescent	apparent	arrogant	assistant
attendance	audience	brilliant	confidence	consistent
convenience	elegant	evidence	fluent	fragrant
frequent	independence	influence	ingredient	instant
insurance	performance	permanent	pleasant	resident

Words ending in *ant*

1. _____ 2. _____ 3. _____
4. _____ 5. _____ 6. _____
7. _____

Words ending in *ent*

8. _____ 9. _____ 10. _____
11. _____ 12. _____ 13. _____
14. _____ 15. _____

Words ending in *ance*

16. _____ 17. _____ 18. _____

Words ending in *ence*

19. _____ 20. _____ 21. _____
22. _____ 23. _____ 24. _____
25. _____

B. In each sentence, one word is spelled incorrectly. Underline the incorrectly spelled words and write them correctly below the sentences.

1. Your assistent seems like an arrogant person.

2. The audience loved the brilliant performance of the lead actor.

3. Only one permanent resident here is an adolescant.

4. How pleasant it is to be in such a fragrent garden!

5. Your attendence has been so consistent that we noticed your absence on Thursday.

6. I love the convenience of instant soup, so it is a frequent ingredient in my cooking.

1. _____ 4. _____
2. _____ 5. _____
3. _____ 6. _____

Spelling Practice 10: Three-Syllable Words

Break longer words into syllables and spell the words by parts. Remember that each syllable contains only one vowel sound. When you see two syllables together in a word, they form two syllables if they stand for separate sounds.

Examples: The word *area* contains three syllables, because the final *e* and *a* stand for separate sounds. The word *reread* contains two syllables, because the final *e* and *a* stand for one sound, long *e*.

A. Write each list word in the space with a slash (/) between the syllables. Use a dictionary if you are unsure where a syllable ends.

Spelling Word

1. accurate _____

2. bulletin _____

3. chemistry _____

4. colossal _____

5. corduroy _____

6. correlate _____

7. creative _____

8. discipline _____

9. exotic _____

10. gallery _____

11. interval _____

12. liable _____

13. magnify _____

14. muscular _____

15. opinion _____

16. oxygen _____

17. parasite _____

18. pelican _____

19. popular _____

20. premium _____

B. Write a word from the list that rhymes with each word below.

1. The name **Mallory** rhymes with _____.

2. The word **robotic** rhymes with _____.

3. The word **dignify** rhymes with _____.

4. The word **dentistry** rhymes with _____.

5. The word **congregate** rhymes with _____.

Spelling Practice 11: Unusual Spellings

Some words have unusual spellings. These spellings must be remembered.

Examples: The word *ecstasy* and *exact* begin with the same sound, but it is spelled differently in each word.

A. Many times, one part of a word has an unusual spelling. Write the word from the spelling list that contains each unusual letter combination shown below.

auxiliary	biscuit	boulder	circuit	colleague
cologne	cordial	dialogue	ecstasy	ghastly
jealous	leisure	leopard	lieutenant	limousine
pageant	parliament	plaid	plateau	protein
sergeant	sovereign	vague	villain	wriggle

Spelling Word

1. ordi   _____
2. eague   _____
3. gha   _____
4. ould   _____
5. eis   _____
6. cstac   _____
7. mous   _____
8. agea   _____
9. teau   _____
10. liam   _____
11. rcuit   _____
12. ague   _____
13. reign   _____
14. wrig   _____
15. ogue   _____
16. lieu   _____
17. jea   _____
18. lain   _____
19. ogne   _____
20. scuit   _____
21. tein   _____
22. liar   _____
23. rgea   _____
24. leop   _____
25. aid   _____

Name _____   Date _____

Spelling Practice 12: Related Words

Some words are related in meaning and spelling. Learning the spelling of one word helps you spell the other.

Examples: The words *child*, *childish*, and *children* are related.

A. Write the two words from the spelling list that are related to each word below.

consume	consumption	deceive	deception	demolish
demolition	denounce	denunciation	illustrative	illustrator
perceive	perception	personal	personality	presume
presumption	pronounce	pronunciation	receive	reception
redeem	redemption	resume	resumption	simplicity
simplify				

Related List Words

1. illustrate   _____   _____

2. deceptive   _____   _____

3. receptor   _____   _____

4. pronouncement   _____   _____

5. denouncing   _____   _____

6. resuming   _____   _____

7. perceptive   _____   _____

8. presumptive   _____   _____

9. consumer   _____   _____

10. simple   _____   _____

11. demolished   _____   _____

12. redeeming   _____   _____

13. personalize   _____   _____

B. In each sentence, one word is spelled incorrectly. Underline the incorrectly spelled words and write them correctly below the sentences.

1. Once we decided to simplify our lives, our consumtion of snack foods dropped.

2. Although I denounce his past actions, he can redeme himself in the future.

3. A good illustrater can change your perception of things.

4. Someone with your personality will find a warm recepsion in that club.

5. I presuem that you plan to demolish that old shack.

6. By using the French pronounciation of that word, you will not deceive anyone.

1. _____   4. _____

2. _____   5. _____

3. _____   6. _____

Spelling Practice 13: Pronunciation and Spelling

Some misspellings are caused by pronunciation. A letter may be silent, or a speaker may drop or add a syllable when saying a word.

Examples: The word *arctic* is often pronounced as if it were spelled *artic*.

A. Write the correct spelling for each misspelled list word below. Circle the letter or letters that were misspelled or omitted originally.

aluminum	arctic	arthritis	athletic	beverage
diamond	different	especially	February	government
governor	library	lightning	literature	miniature
mischievous	nursery	opera	particularly	probably
quantity	restaurant	similarly	vacuum	Wednesday

Spelling Word

1. lightening _____

2. dimond _____

3. miniture _____

4. govenor _____

5. atheletic _____

6. nursry _____

7. Febuary _____

8. probly _____

9. artic _____

10. paticularly _____

11. specially _____

12. restrant _____

13. libary _____

14. vacume _____

15. alumnum _____

16. simlarly _____

17. Wensday _____

18. litrature _____

19. bevrage _____

20. diffrent _____

B. Add to the list in Part A six more words that you think are often misspelled because of pronunciation. First, write them as they are pronounced, and then, write the correct spelling. Use a dictionary if you are unsure of the spelling.

_____ _____ _____ _____ _____ _____

_____ _____ _____ _____ _____ _____

Name _____ Date _____

Spelling Practice 14: Greek Word Roots

Words and word parts from Greek have spellings that must be remembered.

Examples : Greek—khaos   English—chaos

A. Determine whether or not each word is spelled correctly. The Greek words and word parts may help, since the spelling is sometimes similar. Spell incorrect words correctly. Check your spelling in a dictionary.

Spelling Word	Greek	Correct Spelling
1. ciclone	kuklōn	_____
2. awthentic	authentikos	_____
3. anchor	ankura	_____
4. atmisfere	atmos + sphair	_____
5. arial	aero	_____
6. dynamic	dunamikos	_____
7. monerchy	monarkhia	_____
8. tradgedy	tragoidia	_____
9. photagraphy	photo + graphō	_____
10. monatone	monotonus	_____
11. thermistat	thermos + status	_____
12. pnumonia	pneuma	_____
13. catastraphe	katastrophe	_____
14. charicter	kharakter	_____
15. hemisfere	hemi + sphair	_____
16. anynomous	anōnumos	_____
17. rheteric	rhētorikē	_____
18. pantamime	pantomimos	_____
19. thermameter	thermos + metron	_____
20. anphibian	amphibios	_____

B. In each group of words, one word is spelled incorrectly. Underline the incorrectly spelled words and write them correctly in the space provided.

1. monotone	autamatic	amphibian	hemisphere	_____
2. atmosphere	catastrophe	dinamic	cyclone	_____
3. choas	geometry	pantomime	authentic	_____
4. pharmacy	anonymous	photography	tragidy	_____
5. monarchy	ancher	thermometer	rhetoric	_____
6. cylinder	aerial	charactor	pneumonia	_____

Spelling Practice 15: Words with Prefixes, Roots, and Suffixes

Find the prefix, root, or suffix in an unfamiliar word and spell the word by parts.

Examples: The word *immovable* contains a simple prefix, root, and suffix. It is easy to spell when you see that it contains the prefix *im-*, the root *move*, and the suffix *-able*.

A. Write the word from the spelling list that contains the prefix, root, or suffix shown below.

advisable	commitment	construction	disastrous	discouragement
dishonorable	disrespectful	exposure	immobilized	inconspicuous
incredible	indefinite	indigestible	inexcusable	inexhaustible
intermission	intrusion	invention	regardless	remorseful
revolution	semifinalist	undeniable	unpleasantness	untraceable

Spelling Word

1. courage _____
2. definite _____
3. commit _____
4. exhaust _____
5. inter- _____
6. credible _____
7. mobile _____
8. disaster _____
9. invent _____
10. semi- _____
11. expose _____
12. advise _____
13. deny _____
14. respect _____
15. excuse _____
16. revolve _____
17. remorse _____
18. intrude _____
19. trace _____
20. conspicuous _____

B. Add to the list in Part A six additional words that contain one of the prefixes, roots, or suffixes written above.

1. _____   4. _____

2. _____   5. _____

3. _____   6. _____

ANSWERS

ANSWERS

Vocabulary Practice 1: Prefixes (p. 1)

3. abhor
4. i
5. abnormal
6. g
7. averse
8. a
9. avert
10. h
11. becalm
12. b
13. befriend
14. e
15. befuddle
16. c
17. bemoan
18. j
19. bedeck
20. d

Vocabulary Practice 2: Prefixes (p. 2)

A. 1. megabyte
   2. megalith
   3. megaphone
   4. megaton
   5. microbe
   6. microfilm
   7. microorganism
   8. microphone
   9. microscope
   10. microwave
B. 1. megabyte
   2. microscope
   3. microphone
   4. microorganism *or* microbe
   5. megalith
   6. megaphone *or* microphone
   7. megaton
   8. microfilm
   9. microwave
   10. microbe

Vocabulary Practice 3: Prefixes (p. 3)

A. 1. maladjusted
   2. malformed
   3. malpractice
   4. malcontent
   5. malnutrition
B. Possible answers:
   1. one who does good for another
   2. of or relating to a positive or good effect
   3. one who benefits from something; one named to receive moneys from a trust, insurance, or other proceeds
   4. wishing or doing good; generous
   5. hatred; ill will
C. 1. maladjusted
   2. malice
   3. beneficiary
   4. benevolent
   5. malnutrition

Vocabulary Practice 4: Number Prefixes (p. 4)

A. 1. quadruple
   2. sextet
   3. sextuple
   4. octagonal
   5. decade
   6. decathlon
   7. decimal
   8. centennial
   9. centimeter
   10. century
B. 1. octagonal, eight
   2. century, one hundred
   3. centennial, one hundred
   4. sextuple, six
   5. decimal, ten
   6. decathlon, ten
   7. sextet, six
   8. centimeters, one hundred
   9. quadruple, four
   10. decade, ten

Vocabulary Practice 5: Suffixes (p. 5)

A. 1. sympathize
2. visualize
3. paralyze
4. patronize
5. economize
6. analyze
7. idolize
8. mechanize
9. publicize
10. modernize

B. 1. patronize
2. visualize
3. paralyze
4. economize
5. analyze

Vocabulary Practice 6: Suffixes (p. 6)

A. 1. facial
2. conclusive
3. gradual
4. sensual
5. affirmative

B. Possible answers:
1. Protecting a cub is evidence of a mother bear's maternal instinct.
2. The sweetener in this soft drink is artificial.
3. Because Zach is so agile, he gets out of the batter's box quickly.
4. Children seem so passive when they watch television.
5. The lab technician handles the volatile chemicals with great care.

Vocabulary Practice 7: Suffixes (p. 7)

A. 1. alignment
2. indictment
3. acknowledgment
4. inducement
5. achievement

B. 1. environment
2. ornament
3. sentiment
4. temperament
5. predicament

C. 1. environment
2. alignment

3. achievement
4. ornament
5. indictment

Vocabulary Practice 8: Suffixes (p. 8)

A. 1. influential
2. confidential
3. controversial
4. financial
5. commercial

B. Possible answers:
1. Trucks were not allowed to pass through the residential area.
2. There is some superficial explanation in this analysis.
3. Revising is a crucial part of the writing process.
4. The Louisiana Purchase is one of the most substantial land deals ever made.
5. The case must be heard by an impartial judge.

Vocabulary Practice 9: Word Roots (p. 9)

A. Possible answers:
1. sudden
2. penniless
3. evil
4. to disturb; to stop the progress of
5. to burst forth
6. a break; the breaking of bone
7. a piece of, often a small piece from which the whole can only be guessed at
8. a breaking of the rules
9. to stop the progress of
10. a break; often the breaking of the body's soft tissue, such as an internal organ

B. Possible answers:
1. One of the victims in the car accident ruptured her spleen.
2. You will be issued a warning for the first minor infraction of these rules.
3. The fragment of the Greek vase was found by the archaeological team.
4. Please do not disrupt the lecture; there will be time for questions after.
5. The corrupt official took bribes from the businessmen.

Vocabulary Practice 10: Word Roots (p. 10)

A. The following words should be underlined:

portly

portfolio

portable

disposition

rapport

supposition

composite

impostor

proposition

supportive

B. 1. portable
2. supportive
3. portfolio
4. rapport
5. portly
6. supposition
7. proposition
8. impostor
9. disposition
10. composite

Vocabulary Practice 11: Word Roots (p. 11)

Possible answers:

1. to catch, as a disease; legal agreement between two or more parties
2. downcast, depressed, disappointed
3. to take away from in terms of quality or value
4. to pull away someone's attention
5. to send out of or away from; to forcefully or forcibly expel
6. to pull out
7. to put into; to force a fluid into
8. to refuse; to deem unworthy or useless
9. to take back, as a statement; to pull back
10. something sticking out from a surface

B. Possible answers:

1. This lever can be used to eject the material into space.
2. The projection from the roof helped shelter those on the porch.
3. Please don't distract me when I am writing.
4. Aaron felt dejected when he did not make the baseball team.

5. The new screen door detracts from the beauty of that old house.

Vocabulary Practice 12: Word Roots (p. 12)

A. Possible answers:

1. An appendix is "hung" onto the end of the book after everything else comes first.
2. Someone dependable can carry the weight of responsibility.
3. A dependent weighs on, or is a burden to, the person on whom he or she depends.
4. When a pharmacist dispenses medicine, he or she may weigh or count it out.
5. Something expendable is something without much weight or substance, or not worth hanging on to.
6. An expenditure is something you pay out, or weigh out.
7. A pendulum hangs down from a fixed point.
8. A pension is "weighed" out or counted out at fixed intervals.
9. Something perpendicular may hang at a right angle to the horizon.
10. Suspend means "to hang." If you suspend something, like a meeting, you leave it hanging.

B. Possible answers:

1. Draw a line that is perpendicular to this line.
2. Some of the resources were considered to be expendable.
3. The professor was known to dispense advice about careers.
4. Mrs. Florio receives a pension from the state, for which she worked.
5. You can find more information on that topic in the appendix.

Vocabulary Practice 13: Word Roots (p. 13)

A. The following words should be underlined:

antecedents

ancestors

indicate

concede

access

contradict

dictator

interceded

edicts

predecessor

B. 1. access

2. dictator

3. ancestors

4. antecedents

5. indicate

6. intercede

7. concede

8. contradict

9. predecessor

10. edict

Vocabulary Practice 14: Synonyms (p. 14)

A. 1. trite, banal

2. poor, destitute

3. reveal, divulge

4. deception, duplicity

5. excitement, exuberance

6. reject, forswear

7. spoil, indulge

8. control, monopolize

9. sensible, prudent

10. persistent, tenacious

B. 1. prudent

2. forswear

3. duplicity

4. tenacious

5. banal

6. exuberance

7. monopolize

8. indulge

9. divulge

10. destitute

Vocabulary Practice 15: Synonyms (p. 15)

A. 1. highest point, pinnacle

2. creative, innovative

3. bestir, provoke

4. gloomy, morose

5. vulnerable, easily harmed

6. payment, stipend

7. common expression, platitude

8. tarry, delay

9. Adulation, praise

10. impertinent, rude

B. 1. pinnacle

2. morose

3. impertinent

4. tarry

5. stipend

6. platitude

7. vulnerable

8. bestir

9. adulation

10. innovative

Vocabulary Practice 16: Synonyms (p. 16)

A. 1. erroneous

2. fervid

3. delete

4. repel

5. cower

6. forage

7. censure

8. mundane

9. cajole

10. prodigious

B. 1. mundane

2. cower

3. censure

4. delete

5. repel

6. erroneous

7. prodigious

8. forage

9. cajole

10. fervid

Vocabulary Practice 17: Antonyms (p. 17)

A. 1. lethargic

2. pertinent

3. vulgar

4. puerile

5. flippant

6. enmity

7. dilute

8. dormant

9. lenient

10. eminent

B. Possible answers:
1. lazy
2. needed, crucial
3. childish, juvenile
4. hate
5. tasteless, gaudy

Vocabulary Practice 18: Antonyms (p. 18)

A. 1. embrace, rebuff
2. appealing, repugnant
3. foolish, sage
4. befriend, alienate
5. entertaining, tedious
6. opaque, transparent
7. serene, nervous
8. rigid, pliable
9. please, antagonize
10. frank, insincere

B. 1. repugnant
2. alienate
3. rebuff
4. serene
5. sage

Vocabulary Practice 19: Homophones
(p. 19)

A. Possible answers:
1. Both *isle* and *island* begin with *i.*
2. If you canv*ass*, you try to *see* supporters.
3. A coun*sel* might *sell* advice to you.
4. If you're *faint*, you *ain't* feeling good.
5. A p*eer* is almost *exactly equal.*

B. 1. faint
2. pier
3. peer
4. council
5. canvass
6. counsel
7. aisle
8. isle
9. canvas
10. feint

Vocabulary Practice 20: Homophones
(p. 20)

A. Possible answers:

a. The parents gave their assent to the marriage.

b. The ascent to the summit is long and dangerous.

c. The church will hold its annual bazaar on Saturday.

d. Camille looked bizarre with her hair dyed and her face painted.

e. We saw an old cannon at Yorktown, Virginia.

f. Is "Mending Wall" in the canon of American literature?

g. The textures in this decor complement each other.

h. Telling Juana that she was helpful was a welcome compliment.

i. Few people have seen a gorilla in the wild.

j. It is difficult for invading armies to fight against guerrillas on their own territory.

B. 1. bazaar
2. complement
3. canon
4. assent
5. gorilla

Vocabulary Practice 21: Analogies (p. 21)

Answers to part C are shown next to the corresponding items.

A. 1. c. synonym
2. a. antonym
3. b. function
4. a. type
5. c. cause-effect
6. c. part-whole
7. a. type
8. b. function
9. b. type
10. a. antonym

B. 1. b. antonym
2. c. cause-effect
3. a. synonym
4. c. part-whole
5. c. function

Vocabulary Practice 22: Connotations
(p. 22)

Answers may vary. Possible answers are given.

A. 1. a. mediocre
b. normal
c. The **average** film lasts ninety minutes.

2. d. pungent
   e. aromatic
   f. This sweater still carries the **strong** smell of mothballs.
3. g. gaudy
   h. colorful
   i. The **vivid** red attracts birds.
4. j. wavering
   k. open-minded
   l. I am **undecided** about which film to rent.
5. m. notorious
   n. well-known
   o. A **famous** rock star once lived in this house.

B. usual, scented, bright, waffling, noteworthy

Vocabulary Practice 23: Commonly Misused Words (p. 23)

1. a. affect
   b. effect
2. a. apprise
   b. appraise
3. a. averse
   b. adverse
4. a. confidant
   b. confident
5. a. defer
   b. differ
6. a. descent
   b. dissent
7. a. distract
   b. detract
8. a. respectfully
   b. respectively
9. a. conscious
   b. conscience
10. a. excess
    b. access

Vocabulary Practice 24: Commonly Confused Words (p. 24)

Sentences shown are possible answers only.

1. a. flagrant
   b. Those roses are **fragrant**.
2. a. symphony
   b. I feel real **sympathy** for your loss.
3. a. sculptor
   b. The **sculpture** was made of marble.
4. a. static
   b. That number is a guess and not a **statistic**.
5. a. recent
   b. Although I lost, I do not **resent** the woman who won.
6. a. appalling
   b. That lemonade looks very **appealing** on a hot day.
7. a. umpire
   b. The ruler of the **empire** lives far away.
8. a. partition
   b. The students wrote a **petition** asking for a camera club.
9. a. proceed
   b. The lead car will **precede** all the floats and marchers.
10. a. persecute
    b. The district attorney will **prosecute** lawbreakers.

Vocabulary Practice 25: Specialized Vocabulary (p. 25)

A. 1. quarantine
   2. cardiac
   3. sedative or medication
   4. sterile
   5. communicable or contagious
   6. ulcer
   7. medication
   8. dehydration
   9. antidote
   10. insomnia
   11. inoculation
   12. contagious or communicable
   13. hygiene
   14. immunization
   15. epidemic
   16. amnesia
B. 1. yes
   2. yes
   3. no
   4. yes
   5. no

Vocabulary Practice 26: Specialized Vocabulary (p. 26)

A. 1. lien
2. cosigner
3. interest
4. debit
5. collateral
6. withdrawal
7. currency
8. usury
9. liability
10. assets
11. foreclose
12. creditor

B. 1. diversified; variety; a term often used to describe an investment strategy that allows losses in one sector of the market to be offset with investments in another sector of the market
2. annuity; an investment that provides regular payments over the buyer's lifetime
3. investment; money spent for income or profit
4. unsecured; not guaranteed by any property used as security
5. maturity; the date when a loan, note, or bond is due

Vocabulary Practice 27: Specialized Vocabulary (p. 27)

A. 1. gourmet
2. resume
3. masquerade
4. mirage
5. naive
6. rendezvous
7. debut
8. fillet
9. boutique
10. intrigue
11. charade
12. souvenir
13. blase
14. entree
15. chaperone
16. debris

B. 1. no
2. yes
3. yes
4. yes
5. no

Vocabulary Practice 28: Specialized Vocabulary (p. 28)

A. 1. coup
2. despot
3. antiquity
4. abdicate
5. neutrality
6. coalition
7. pacifist
8. amnesty
9. anarchy
10. inauguration

B. 1. dynasty
2. medieval
3. depose
4. totalitarian
5. disarmament
6. contemporary
7. feudalism
8. renaissance

Vocabulary Practice 29: Specialized Vocabulary (p. 29)

A. 1. fjord
2. mesa or plateau
3. isthmus
4. plateau
5. delta
6. reservoir
7. cartographer
8. tundra
9. irrigation
10. urban
11. arid
12. uninhabitable
13. prairie
14. seismology
15. nomad

B. 1. yes
2. no
3. no
4. yes
5. yes

Spelling Practice 1: Short and Long Vowel Spellings (p. 30)

A. The following words should be written in the Long Vowel column. Marked letters should be circled:

1. acqu**ai**nt
2. c**ea**se
4. conc**ea**l
5. ebon**y**
6. er**o**de
7. evapor**a**te
8. gr**a**teful
10. h**u**mid
11. h**y**drant
12. imp**ea**ch
14. l**ea**flet
15. m**ea**sles
18. portr**ay**
19. prom**o**te
21. sch**e**me

These words should appear in the Short Vowel column.

3. clutter
9. hectic
13. intelligent
16. mimic
17. phantom
20. pulse
22. shingle
23. stamina
24. strengthen
25. trinket

B. 1. conceal
2. evaporate
3. impeach
4. acquaint
5. scheme
6. trinket

Spelling Practice 2: Digraphs (p. 31)

A. The following words should be written in the Word Spelled Correctly column. Marked letters should be in the Digraph column:

A. 1. **aw**kward
4. cart**oo**n
5. c**au**liflower
7. comp**ou**nd
8. depl**oy**
9. dev**ou**r
10. dil**ute**
12. f**au**cet
13. fl**ou**nder
14. gr**ou**chy
15. h**au**ghty
16. h**oi**st
18. iss**ue**
19. n**oi**sy
20. prof**ou**nd
22. rec**oi**l
23. sc**ou**ndrel
24. t**ea**spoon
25. tr**ou**t

B. 1. chowder
2. duplex
3. intrude
4. booster
5. bough
6. dilute

Spelling Practice 3: Vowels before r (p. 32)

A. Words containing **ar**

1. carpenter
2. carpeting
3. carton
4. malaria
5. mortar
6. partial
7. scar
8. varnish

Words containing **er**

9. detergent
10. furthermore
11. insert
12. inverted
13. mercy
14. merely
15. superb

Words containing **or**

16. authority
17. dormitory
18. forfeit
19. furthermore
20. glorious

21. mortar
22. porpoise

Words containing **ir** or **ur** or a digraph plus **r**

23. dirty
24. disturbance
25. flourish
26. furnace
27. furthermore
28. impaired

B. Possible Answers:

smart, heart, shirt, burnish, floor, tarnish

Spelling Practice 4: Double and Single Consonants (p. 33)

A. The following words should be written in the **One** column:

1. aggravate
3. boycott
4. broccoli
5. channel
8. exaggerate
9. excess
10. immense
11. innocent
13. mayonnaise
14. occasion
16. pennant
18. procession
19. recommend
20. scissors
21. surrender
22. tariff
23. territory
24. trespass

The following words should be written in the **Two** column:

2. assassin
6. committee
7. embarrass
12. mattress
15. occurrence
17. possession
25. unnecessary

B. 1. assassin
2. committee
3. embarrass
4. occurrence

5. trespass
6. unnecessary

Spelling Practice 5: Compound Words (p. 34)

A. 1. back, pack
2. beehive, bee, hive
3. breakthrough, break, through
4. briefcase, brief, case
5. copy, right
6. count, down
7. dining room, dining, room
8. double, cross
9. far, fetched
10. key, board
11. newsstand, news, stand
12. nonetheless, none, the, less
13. not, with, standing
14. out, of, date
15. oversight, over, sight
16. quick, witted
17. saddlebag, saddle, bag
18. self, esteem
19. self-taught, self, taught
20. study, hall
21. teenager, teen, ager
22. text, book
23. three-fourths, three, fourths
24. thumbnail, thumb, nail
25. yardstick, yard, stick

B. The words shown should be underlined in the sentences.

1. dining room
2. study hall
3. keyboard
4. quick-witted
5. self-taught
6. three-fourths

Spelling Practice 6: Unstressed Endings (p. 35)

A. Words ending in **al**

1. arrival
2. betrayal
3. decimal
4. editorial
5. industrial

6. journal
7. liberal
8. manual
9. original
10. rational

Words ending in **le**

11. ankle
12. article
13. beetle
14. entangle
15. hustle
16. startle
17. steeple
18. wrestle

Words ending in **ar, el, in,** or **or**

19. author
20. conqueror
21. mirror
22. quarrel
23. scholar
24. spectacular
25. uncertain

B. 1. manual
2. author
3. quarrel
4. decimal
5. arrival
6. mirror

Spelling Practice 7: Syllable Patterns (p. 36)

A. 1. plunger VCCV
2. bonus; longVCV
3. campus, VCCV
4. VCCV
5. crimson, VCCV
6. VCCV
7. devout, shortVCV
8. donor, long VCV
9. VCCV
10. VCCV
11. excuse, VCCV
12. long VCV
13. gallop, VCCV
14. VCCV
15. VCCV
16. quota, long VCV

17. rumor, long VCV
18. VCCV
19. slogan, long VCV
20. suspense, VCCV
21. VCCV
22. vengeance, VCCV
23. venom, short VCV
24. VCCV
25. witness, VCCV

B. Possible Answers

VCCV: wrapper, differ, portal

long V/CV   motion, timing, racing

short VC/V   comet, suburb, rebel

Spelling Practice 8: Adding Suffixes (p. 37)

A. 1. acquitted   acquit + ed
2. bubbling   bubble + ing
3. certified   certify + ed
4. challenging   challenge + ing
5. comedian   comedy + an
6. controlling   control + ing
7. corroded   corrode + ed
8. criticized   criticize + ed
9. democratic   democrat + ic
10. denied   deny + ed
11. divisible   divide + ible
12. evolving   evolve + ing
13. fascinating   fascinate + ing
14. historical   history + ical
15. mystified   mystify + ed
16. occupied   occupy + ed
17. patrolling   patrol + ing
18. pitied   pity + ed
19. pledging   pledge + ing
20. preferred   prefer + ed
21. pried   pry + ed
22. pursuing   pursue + ing
23. reducible   reduce + ible
24. regretted   regret + ed
25. sturdiest   sturdy + est

B. Possible Answers

approval   approve + al

plentiful   plenty + ful

allotted   allot + ed

Spelling Practice 9: More Unstressed Endings (p. 38)

A. Words ending in **ant**

1. arrogant
2. assistant
3. brilliant
4. elegant
5. fragrant
6. instant
7. pleasant

Words ending in **ent**

8. adolescent
9. apparent
10. consistent
11. fluent
12. frequent
13. ingredient
14. permanent
15. resident

Words ending in **ance**

16. attendance
17. insurance
18. performance

Words ending in **ence**

19. absence
20. audience
21. confidence
22. convenience
23. evidence
24. independence
25. influence

B. 1. assistant
2. performance
3. adolescent
4. fragrant
5. attendance
6. ingredient

Spelling Practice 10: Three-Syllable Words (p. 39)

A. 1. ac / cu / rate
2. bul / le / tin
3. chem / is / try
4. co / los / sal
5. cor / du / roy
6. co r/ re / late

7. cre / a / tive
8. dis / ci / pline
9. ex / o / tic
10. ga / ler / y
11. in / ter / val
12. li / a / ble
13. mag / ni / fy
14. mus /cu / lar
15. o / pin / ion
16. ox / y / gen
17. par / a / site
18. pel / i / can
19. pop / u / lar
20. pre / mi /um
21. sal / a / ry
22. spe / cial / ize
23. sum / ma / rize
24. tour / na / ment
25. vet / er / an

B. 1. gallery, salary
2. exotic
3. magnify
4. chemistry
5. correlate
6. opinion

Spelling Practice 11: Unusual Spellings (p. 40)

A. 1. cordial
2. colleague
3. ghastly
4. boulder
5. leisure
6. ecstasy
7. limousine
8. pageant
9. plateau
10. parliament
11. circuit
12. vague
13. sovereign
14. wriggle
15. dialogue
16. lieutenant
17. jealous
18. villain
19. cologne

20. biscuit
21. protein
22. auxiliary
23. sergeant
24. leopard
25. plaid
B. 1. leisure
2. protein
3. dialogue
4. ecstasy
5. colleague
6. vague

Spelling Practice 12: Related Words (p. 41)
A. Words may appear in reversed order.
1. illustrative, illustrator
2. deceive, deception
3. receive, reception
4. pronounce, pronunciation
5. denounce, denunciation
6. resume, resumption
7. perceive, perception
8. presume, presumption
9. consume, consumption
10. simplicity, simplify
11. demolish, demolition
12. redeem, redemption
13. personal, personality
B. 1. consumption
2. redeem
3. illustrator
4. reception
5. presume
6. pronunciation

Spelling Practice 13: Pronunciation and Spelling (p. 42)
A. Marked letters or those nearby should be circled.
1. ligh**tn**ing
2. di**a**mond
3. min**ia**ture
4. gov**er**nor
5. a**thl**etic
6. nur**ser**y
7. Feb**r**uary
8. pro**ba**bly

9. ar**c**tic
10. pa**r**ticularly
11. **e**specially
12. rest**au**rant
13. lib**r**ary
14. vac**uu**m
15. alum**in**um
16. sim**i**larly
17. We**d**nesday
18. lit**e**rature
19. bev**e**rage
20. diff**e**rent
21. gover**n**ment
22. mischie**v**ous
23. arthri**tis**
24. quan**ti**ty
25. op**e**ra
B. Possible Answers
seprately/separately,
sophmore/sophomore,
undoubtally/undoubtedly,
dignose/diagnose,
contempery/contemporary,
libral/liberal

Spelling Practice 14: Greek Word Roots (p. 43)
A. 1. cyclone
2. authentic
3. [blank]
4. atmosphere
5. aerial
6. [blank]
7. monarchy
8. tragedy
9. photography
10. monotone
11. thermostat
12. pneumonia
13. catastrophe
14. character
15. hemisphere
16. anonymous
17. rhetoric
18. pantomime
19. thermometer
20. amphibian

21. [blank]
22. geometry
23. pharmacy
24. automatic
25. cylinder

B. 1. automatic
2. dynamic
3. chaos
4. tragedy
5. anchor
6. character

Spelling Practice 15: Words with Prefixes, Roots, and Suffixes (p. 44)

A. 1. discouragement
2. indefinite
3. commitment
4. inexhaustible
5. intermission
6. incredible
7. immobilized
8. disastrous
9. invention
10. semifinalist
11. exposure
12. advisable
13. undeniable
14. disrespectful
15. inexcusable
16. revolution
17. remorseful
18. intrusion
19. untraceable
20. inconspicuous
21. indigestible
22. construction
23. dishonorable
24. regardless
25. unpleasantness

B. Possible Answers
1. courageous
2. uncommitted
3. mobilization
4. digestion
5. respectfully
6. hopeless